Opposites

Night and Day

Siân Smith

Raintree is an imprint of Capstone Global Library
Limited, a company incorporated in England and
Wales having its registered office at 7 Pilgrim Street,
London, EC4V 6LB – Registered company number:
6695582

www.raintreepublishers.co.uk
myorders@raintreepublishers.co.uk

Edited by Siân Smith, Diyan Leake, and Brynn Baker
Designed by Tim Bond and Peggie Carley
Picture research by Liz Alexander
Production by Victoria Fitzgerald
Originated by Capstone Global Library Ltd
Printed and bound in China

ISBN 978 1 406 28304 4
18 17 16 15 14
10 9 8 7 6 5 4 3 2 1

British Library Cataloguing in Publication Data
A full catalogue record for this book is available from
the British Library.

Acknowledgements
We would like to thank the following for permission
to reproduce photographs: Alamy: © all, 10, © Kirk
Norbury, 12, 23b, front cover left, 23b, © Piotr Skubisz,
front cover right, © T.Walker / Photri Images, 13, ©
Valerio Agolino, 7; Corbis: Glenn Bartley/All Canada
Photos, 14; Getty Image: Dennis McColeman, 20,
JGI/Jamie Grill, 8, Rubberball/Mark Andersen, 15;
Shutterstock: 2xSamara.com, 4, 22a, djgis, 5, Goodluz, 9,
Olga_Phoenix, 21, pisaphotography, 6, Sergey Novikov,
11, back cover bottom, Songquan Deng, 16, back
cover top, SuperStock: Ableimages, 18

Every effort has been made to contact copyright
holders of material reproduced in this book. Any
omissions will be rectified in subsequent printings if
notice is given to the publisher.

Contents

Day and night

It is **day**.

We can see the Sun.

It is **night**.

We can see the Moon.

Day

We can see sunshine.

We can eat.

We can go shopping.

We can play.

Night

We can see the stars.

We can see bats.

We can see owls.

We can go to sleep.

Is this day or night?

This is night.

Is this day or night?

This
is
day.

Day and night poem

The light of the Sun
wakes up everyone.
The Moon's gone away,
it must be day!

The Moon's in the sky,
and bats flutter by.
There isn't much light,
it must be night!

Picture glossary

day the time between sunrise and sunset, when it is light

night the time between sunset and sunrise, when it is dark

Index

Notes for teachers and parents

BEFORE READING

Building background:

Ask children what they see when they look up at the night sky. What time do they wake up in the morning? What do they see in the sky then?

AFTER READING

Recall and reflection:

Which animals might we see or hear in the night (bats and owls)? Explain that these animals are nocturnal. What are some of the things we do in the day?

Sentence knowledge:

Help children find pages with questions. How do they know?

Word knowledge (phonics):

Encourage children to point at the word *day* on any page. Sound out the phonemes in the word *d/ay.* Ask children to sound out each phoneme as they point at the letters and then blend the sounds together to make the word *day.* Challenge them to say some words that rhyme with *day* (may, pay, ray, way).

Word recognition:

Ask children to point at the word *night* on any page.

AFTER-READING ACTIVITIES

In a dark room, shine a torch on a mirror and direct the reflected light on to a surface such as a cupboard door. Explain that the torch is like the Sun and the mirror is like the Moon. The light from the mirror is just a reflection of the light from the torch.

In this book

Topic

day and night

Sentence stems

1. This is ___ .
2. We can see the ___ .
3. Is this ___ or ___ ?
4. It is ___ .

High-frequency words

and	of
be	or
by	see
can	the
day	there
go	this
in	to
is	up
it	we